T0209293

The
Prayer
DIGEST

Inspired Prayers with Fresh
Biblical Insights

CAROL ANN BOYD

WESTBOW
PRESS®
A DIVISION OF THOMAS NELSON
& ZONDERVAN

Copyright © 2023 Carol Ann Boyd.

All rights reserved. No part of this book may be used or reproduced by any means, graphic, electronic, or mechanical, including photocopying, recording, taping or by any information storage retrieval system without the written permission of the author except in the case of brief quotations embodied in critical articles and reviews.

WestBow Press books may be ordered through booksellers or by contacting:

WestBow Press
A Division of Thomas Nelson & Zondervan
1663 Liberty Drive
Bloomington, IN 47403
www.westbowpress.com
844-714-3454

Because of the dynamic nature of the Internet, any web addresses or links contained in this book may have changed since publication and may no longer be valid. The views expressed in this work are solely those of the author and do not necessarily reflect the views of the publisher, and the publisher hereby disclaims any responsibility for them.

Any people depicted in stock imagery provided by Getty Images are models, and such images are being used for illustrative purposes only. Certain stock imagery © Getty Images.

Scripture taken from the King James Version of the Bible.

Art and Graphics approved by Myron J. Boyd II, Dallas, GA.

ISBN: 978-1-6642-8946-8 (sc)
ISBN: 978-1-6642-8947-5 (hc)
ISBN: 978-1-6642-8945-1 (e)

Library of Congress Control Number: 2023900974

Print information available on the last page.

WestBow Press rev. date: 7/27/2023

DEDICATION

To the memory of my best friend and loving husband of forty-two years, the Honorable Bishop Melvin Boyd, with deep love and affection. He is the reason for my passion to write this book.

CONTENTS

ACKNOWLEDGMENTS

To Bishop Theodore Brooks, the presiding Bishop of the Pentecostal Assemblies of the World, Inc. He is a devoted spiritual leader and prayer warrior. His core values have impacted the lives of many people. The board of bishops and lay members stands in solidarity with his wisdom and excellent leadership.

To my devoted family. They are always supportive of my music, singing, writing, and biblical teaching.

To Dr. Willa Moore; a friend, mentor, and woman of notable wisdom. She is the epitome of elegance and grace.

To my niece, Faye Clemmons, for her dutiful, meticulous, and tireless editing skills, without which I would not have been able to publish this book.

To my daughter, Monica Howse, for managing my book project and handling all of the publishing details.

FOREWORD

In an Age when there is a proliferation of books and a scarcity of substance, it is difficult to approach another text without reflecting on the words of King Solomon, And further, by these, my son, be admonished: of making many books there is no end, and much study is a weariness of the flesh" (Ecclesiastes 12:12 KJV). The last thing the world, the church, you, or I need is another irrelevant book—one that does more to enlarge an author's ego than to edify a hungry reader. I wish to assure you, dear reader, that what you are holding in your hands is not just "another book."

I can say that because *The Prayer Digest* calls us to engage in the most important of human endeavors: prayer. In this work, the author, Lady Carol Boyd, doesn't just call us to pray more. Rather, she offers us guidance and companionship as we explore the requirements and benefits of prayer. She offers us not just her own experiences, but clear insights from the word of God.

I can attest that this is not just another book because I have had the privilege of knowing the author for over four decades. We have shared the same vocation: wives supporting and serving in the ministry alongside our husbands, both of whom pioneered thriving churches. Ours is a unique calling that requires broad shoulders and a broader set of skills. Being a "leading lady" is more than just being a wife to a prominent pastor or leader; it involves being a sounding board, co-visionary, confidant, hostess, unpaid counselor, and most importantly, a prayer warrior. Mrs. Boyd has lived the life she writes about. I have had the opportunity to observe her across the years as she co-labored with her late husband, the Honorable Bishop Melvin Boyd, in building the Grace Apostolic Church in Nashville, Tennessee.

More than just an accomplished author, she was the church organist, sharing her gifts not only in the local arena but in the international one as well. She has succeeded in rearing seven spirit-filled, talented children who are all active in the ministry. I have seen her weather the adversity of the untimely passing of her husband. She is able to maintain her poise and equilibrium in the most difficult of times because of her spiritual roots—her real and vibrant prayer life.

It is from her perspective of faith that she is able to draw the authority and credibility needed to present this book. When she speaks of the power and purpose of prayer, she is not sharing something she heard, but something she has lived. She invites us—her readers—to form a closer relationship with God, who hears and answers our prayers. If you answer her invitation to draw closer to God through prayer, you will encounter the secrets of strength that have sustained praying believers through time immemorial. And so, I say this is not "another book" but an encounter!

Affectionately submitted,
Mother Willa M. Moore, DHL

CAROL ANN BOYD

PREFACE

The purpose of this book is to share my thoughts and experiences, lend guidance, and give a biblical approach to prayer. In these pages, I present reasons and various ways to communicate with God. The first mention of prayer in the bible is found in **Genesis 4:26 (KJV), which states, "men began to call upon the name of the Lord."** Shouldn't we, as the people of God, call on his name today? I hope you will connect to the Creator and align yourself to his will through prayer and reading his word.

Prayer is more than a petition, and God is not a magic genie. Prayer is communion with God. The songwriter Joseph C. Ludgate wrote "Friendship with Jesus, fellowship divine, oh what blessed sweet communion, Jesus is a friend of mine." Prayer should be more than a casual dialogue between you and God. Prayer should not be sporadic but often. Daily prayer is challenging but highly beneficial. Prayer will bring about continual life changes and help us maintain our integrity before God and man.

This book is a compilation of prayers categorized under various headings. It also includes a "speaker's source" section that gives fresh insight and illustrates practical life applications for these prayers.

In God's word, we are both instructed and invited to pray. I hope this book will inspire you to lift your heart in prayer to God.

CAROL ANN BOYD

The Requirements of Prayer

One must know what is required or necessary for prayer. Below, I list the actions one should take to successfully pray.

1. Direct your prayer to God (Philippians 4:6)
2. Come boldly (Hebrew 4:16)
3. Stand praying, forgive (Mark 11:25)
4. Ask in faith (Mark 11:24; Hebrew 11:6)
5. Be Specific (Mark 10:51)

The Benefits of Prayer

Prayer is our means of communicating with our Creator. It's like referring to the manufacturer's manual for instructions and guidance. Communicating with our maker helps us to navigate our lives from the Creator's perspective.

Healing

2 Chronicles 7:14; James 5:16

1. Accentuate the positive. Corporative prayer enhances the power of the Holy Ghost (Acts 4:31)

2. Expectation (Jeremiah 29:11, 31:17; Psalm 62:5)

3. Perfect peace (Isaiah 26:3)

4. The criteria for inner peace is to stay connected to God by prayer and reading the word

Prayer Menu and Options

A Prayer Menu (a list of available choices) is a suggestion to focus on specific needs, desires, and choices. The people of God, when praying, should never be nonchalant and generalizing. We must not make vague or indefinite requests that appear to be indifferent and show a lack of genuine concern. When the server asks what they can get you at a restaurant, who replies with, "Whatever you have." Why should one pray, "Any way you bless me, I'll be satisfied"?

Ye lust, and have not: ye kill, and desire to have, and cannot obtain: ye fight and war, yet ye have not, because ye ask not. (James 4:2 KJV)

If any of you lack wisdom, let him ask of God, that giveth to all men liberally, and upbraideth not; and it shall be given him. (James 1:5 KJV)

Ask, and it shall be given you; seek, and ye shall find; knock, and it shall

CAROL ANN BOYD

be opened unto you: For everyone that asketh receiveth; and he that seeketh findeth, and to him that knocketh it shall be opened.Or what man is there of you, whom if his son asks bread, will he give him a stone?Or if he ask a fish, will he give him a serpent? If ye then, being evil, know how to give good gifts unto your children, how much more shall your Father which is in heaven give good things to them that ask him? (Matthew 7:7–11 KJV)

We have not because we ask not!

SELECTIVE PRAYER

There are menus from which one chooses in a restaurant; however, the waiter (preacher) may suggest items that might interest you and appeal to your taste buds. When the waiter asks, "What can I get for you?" it is an opportunity to ask for something that may not be printed on the menu. Just because it isn't printed or displayed on the menu, does not mean you can't ask for it and order it. One must believe to see. Remember what **Mark 9:23b says: "All things are possible to him that believeth."**

THE IMPOTENT MAN AT THE POOL OF BETHESDA

When Jesus saw him lie, and knew that he had been now a long time in that case, he saith unto him, Wilt thou be made whole? The impotent man answered him. Sir, I have no man, when the water is troubled, to put me into the pool: but while I am coming, another steppeth down before me. (John 5:6–7 KJV)

Jesus gave the lame man an option and asked (as a waiter would ask) what would you like? "Wilt thou be made whole?"

CAROL ANN BOYD

Just because you can't see a possible way out of your situation does not mean there is no way. You must ask and believe you will receive what you have requested.

Precision Prayers

*Being precise in prayer gets results!
You should be specific, detailed, and
exact about every request.*

And behold, two blind men sitting by the road, when they heard that Jesus was passing by, cried out, saying, "Have mercy on us, O Lord, Son of David!" Then the multitude warned them that they should be quiet; but they cried out all the more, saying, "Have mercy on us, O Lord, Son of David!" So Jesus stood still and called them, and said, "What do you want Me to do for you?" They said to Him, "Lord, that our eyes may be opened." So Jesus had compassion and touched their eyes. And immediately their eyes received sight, and they followed Him. (Matthew 20: 30–34 KJV)

BARTIMAEUS

And they came to Jericho: and as he went out of Jericho with his disciples and a great number of people, blind Bartimaeus, the son of Timaeus, sat by the highway side begging. And when he heard that it was Jesus of Nazareth,

CAROL ANN BOYD

he began to cry out, and say, Jesus, thou Son of David, have mercy on me. And many charged him that he should hold his peace: but he cried the more a great deal, Thou Son of David, have mercy on me. And Jesus stood still and commanded him to be called. And they call the blind man, saying unto him, be of good comfort, rise; he calleth thee. And he, casting away his garment, rose and came to Jesus. And Jesus answered and said unto him, what wilt thou that I should do unto thee? The blind man said unto him, Lord, that I might receive my sight. And Jesus said unto him, Go thy way; thy faith hath made thee whole. And immediately he received his sight and followed Jesus in the way. (Mark 10:46–52 KJV)

(It appears that asking is a sign of faith.)

THE PRAYER OF JABEZ

And Jabez called on the God of Israel, saying, Oh that thou would bless me indeed, and enlarge my coast, and that thine hand might be with me, and that thou wouldest keep me from evil, that it may not grieve me! And God granted him that which he requested. (1 Chronicles 4:10 KJV)

THE SYROPHOENICIAN WOMAN (CAN I HAVE A CRUMB?)

For a certain woman, whose young daughter had an unclean spirit, heard of him, and came and fell at his feet: The woman was a Greek, a Syrophenician by nation; and she besought him that he would cast forth the devil out of her daughter. She did not get the crumb until after she said, "yes Lord." Yes, to whatever the Lord says. Ask God to put a yes in your spirit. I'll say "yes, Lord!

CAROL ANN BOYD

Yes, to Your will and to Your way." But Jesus said unto her, Let the children first be filled: for it is not meet to take the children's bread and to cast it unto the dogs. And she answered and said unto him, Yes, Lord: yet the dogs under the table eat of the children's crumbs. And he said unto her, For this saying go thy way; the devil is gone out of thy daughter. And when she was come to her house, she found the devil was gone out, and her daughter laid upon the bed. (Mark 7:25–30 KJV)

You must recognize that the kingdom and all the power belong to God forever and through all eternity.

Inspirational Prayers

*The following prayers were written
to motivate and uplift believers.*

PASTORS AND MINISTERS

~ *Let us Pray* ~

Heavenly Father, you are the great shepherd. We ask you to direct and undergird your pastors and ministers by the power of the Holy Ghost and give them a spiritual fervor for souls. You gave us pastors after your heart. Guide your servant to feed the sheep with knowledge and understanding through your word. Release in your servant a fresh anointing, and a renewed desire to carry out your will.

Inspire your servant with divine wisdom and cause them to speak under the auspices of the Holy Ghost. Cause them to set their face like a flint, and not fear faces, but cry aloud and lift their voices like a trumpet in Zion.

HEALING

God desires us to be healthy and whole, both physically and spiritually. I pray that you are inspired to pray for your physical, spiritual, and mental healing as you read the scripture examples below.

> **God is not a man, that he should lie; neither the son of man, that he should repent: hath he said, and shall he not do it? Or hath he spoken, and shall he not make it good? (Numbers 23:19 KJV)**

> **Who forgiveth all thine iniquities; who healeth all thy diseases. (Psalm 103:3 KJV)**

> **But unto you, that fear my name shall the Sun of righteousness arise with healing in his wings, and ye shall go forth and grow up as calves of the stall. (Malachi 4:2 KJV)**

~ Let us Pray ~

Oh Lord, our Lord, how excellent is thy name in all the earth! We ask you, holy God and sun of righteous, to arise with healing in your wings, for by your stripes we are healed. Our eyes are upon you and we look to you to perform your perfect word. We believe, that if you said it, you will do it. You are not a man and cannot lie.

By the power of the Holy Ghost invested in me, I command sickness and disease to leave the body. We speak life into dead situations. We command depression to go. You are the potter; we are the clay to be molded after your will. Heal the brokenhearted and broken spirits and cause us to come under alignment with your divine will.

Now unto the King eternal, immortal, invisible, the only wise God, be honor and glory forever and ever. Amen! (1 Timothy 1:17 KJV)

TRUSTING GOD

Trust in God isn't automatic. It is something that must be practiced and lived out daily. During times of uncertainty, we must reflect on times when God carried us through similar experiences. We must rely on his word to see us through difficult times. The bible says that God honors his word above his name (Psalm 138:2 KJV). The more you work toward trusting him, the easier it will become!

What time I am afraid I will trust in thee. (Psalm 56:3 KJV)

~ Let us Pray ~

Thank you for giving us hope, for it is the anchor of our souls. We trust you. Our hopes and dreams are in you. We put everything into your hands. You are our rock, our sword and shield, and our high tower. Lord, you are our battle axe and buckler and always our bridge over troubled waters.

When the vicissitudes of life are beyond our control and situations shock us, the Holy Ghost within us is our shock absorber. We trust you to be our shelter in the time of storm. You are our strong deliverer. You are the mighty one. You are our inspector, our director, and our divine protector. You are the fence around us every day. Lord, you are our keeper, and we are not afraid. You are both sunlight and shade.

Your all-seeing eye is upon us. Your heart is turned toward us. We ask you to promote our love, for there is no fear in perfect love. In your name we rebuke fear and doubt; we cast out depression and discouragement.

We believe you, and we trust you. We pray that you will make your face shine upon us. And we will go forth this day in the power of your great name, Jesus. Glory, honor, dominion, and power belong to you. Amen and amen.

PRAYER FOR THE GRIEVING

Grieving the loss of a loved one or of something that has been removed from your life can be very challenging and devastating, but you should understand that grief is a natural process.

I recently suffered the loss of my husband of forty-two years. My husband and I married right out of high school and began our life together. He became a pastor and pastored for thirty-three years. For all of my adult life, all I knew was being married and being a pastor's wife. I knew nothing about living a life apart from my husband.

I know what it means to hear the lack of noise from being alone and having to make decisions by yourself. I know what it's like to pay bills by yourself, eat in restaurants alone, travel solo, and be approached by widowed men.

Going to church and was a reminder that my husband was no longer there.

It was after my husband's death that I had to learn to rely on God and trust him to lead and guide me into this life unknown. It was during this time that my relationship with God grew stronger through prayer and reading his word.

So, if you are struggling with grief today, I encourage you to draw near to God through prayer and reading his word.

~ Let us Pray ~

Heavenly Father, we pray for all those who feel sorrow and grief over the recent passing of a special loved one. Please lift them above the shadows of despair and place the rays of sunlight into their hearts. Please comfort all those in mourning and deep sadness today. Lift every bowed head. Strengthen the weak and mend their broken hearts. I pray that you refresh and renew the minds of those who are deeply disturbed. Almighty God, please lift every heavy burden. Earth has no sorrow that you cannot heal. You give victory in the face of defeat, and joy in the midst of sorrow.

Oh, Lord, please gather the poor in spirit into your loving arms. Cover and protect them with your blood. Embrace the fearful with your peace. Let them know your compassion and feel your kindness and tender care. May they put their hope and trust in you, always and forever. In the blessed name of Jesus, amen, and amen!

CAROL ANN BOYD

SEEKING GOD'S HELP

Seeking God's help requires action on the part of the believer. This should be a two-way conversation between you and God.

> **There is none like unto the God of Jeshurun, who rideth upon the heaven in thy help, and in his excellency on the sky. (Deuteronomy 33:26 KJV)**

~ Let us Pray ~

Lord, please stretch forth your mighty hand toward us and send help from your sanctuary.

Give us help from trouble: for vain is the help of man. (Psalm 60:11 KJV)

Some trust in chariots, and some in horses: but we will remember the name of the Lord our God. (Psalm 20:7 KJV)

Oh, God, move on your throne. Oh, God, our rock of ages, hide us in the cleft of the rock. We come boldly to the throne so that we may obtain your profound mercy and find grace to help us in our times of need.

Lord, we seek your help while you can be found.

You were our help in ages past, and you are our hope in the years to come. We thank you today, Lord, for being our present help during troubled times. In *everything,* we give you thanks, for this is your will. We bless you at *all times.* We seek to do your will and praise you for your present help. We give you glory and honor in your blessed name, Jesus, amen and amen!

PRAYING THE WORD

Praying God's word is simply reminding God of what he's already said. It is impossible to remind God of his word if you don't know his word. Prayer and reading scriptures go hand in hand.

> **My people are destroyed for lack of knowledge. (Hosea 4:6 KJV)**

> **And the Lord shall make thee the head, and not the tail, and thou shalt be above only, and thou shalt not be beneath. (Deuteronomy 28:13 KJV)**

WORD DECLARATIONS

~ Let us Pray ~

Lord, you said if our ways please you, we can ask what we will from you. We pray now according to your word, and your word is perfect, tried, and true. Your word is pure.

Jesus, you are the king of kings and lord of lords. Our crosses to bear are not greater than your grace. You will not allow us to be tempted more than we can handle. You promised to never forsake us. We are not alone. You are forever at our side. Oh, God, rock us in the cradle of your loving arms.

Lord God, we pray your word. You have given us the power to decree a thing, and it shall be established. So, Lord, we declare freedom, and we are released today from worry, depression, and anxiety, for your word tells us to be anxious about nothing, but pray about everything. Your word says we are to cast all our cares upon you, for you care for us.

And so today, we speak peace over our lives, we speak healing over our bodies, for your word says by your stripes we are healed. We speak financial blessings, for your word declares the cattle of a thousand hills are yours. Your word says we are the head, and not the tail.

Lord, we believe your word. Your word is perfect, tried, and true. You are the same God that hung the earth on the periphery of nothing, brought the cosmos out of chaos, and created us from the earth, and we are healed by your divine power.

Today we bless you and praise you. Your praise is always in our mouths. We give you all the glory and honor, now and forever. In Jesus's name, amen and amen.

GRATEFULNESS

Merriam-Webster defines gratefulness as being appreciative of the benefits received. Being grateful is about not taking things for granted, but rather being thankful for what we have already received and for what we're about to receive. Gratefulness is a powerful tool for connecting with God. It is with this understanding that we should have a grateful attitude during prayer.

~ Let us Pray ~

Lord Jesus, thank you for waking us up in our right minds with the ability to think and make wise decisions. Thank you for the activity in our limbs. It was not the alarm clock, TV, or radio that allowed us to open our eyes. It was your grace and mercy, and we are so grateful. Thank you for giving us a brand-new day and brand-new mercy. Thank you for giving us another chance to serve you as our God and king. Thank you for watching over us all through the night while we sleep. We are truly grateful, and may we embrace every opportunity to help others this day. We bless your high name, Jesus! Amen.

CAROL ANN BOYD

PRAISE AND ADORATION

The word says that God inhabits the praises of his people, so let's begin our prayer by giving God the praise, honor, and adoration that he's due.

~ Let us Pray ~

God of wisdom, power, and might, we humbly bow before you. How excellent and majestic is your name. There is none higher than you. You are glorious in all your majesty and power. You ride the wind and control the storms on the sea of life. You are almighty. You make the ocean waves lie down at your command, and they are still. You speak peace to our stormy situations. You calm our anxieties, and our fears subside. You make our spirits strong. When the enemy comes in like a flood, you are the Lord and highest judge. You lift up a standard and issue a restraining order against our fierce enemy. Every weapon that is formed against us will fail. So we bow before you and praise you for your power and might. You are the king of glory. You are our lord, strong and mighty. You are mighty in battle. And now, Lord, we give you all the glory and honor that is due to your great name. Amen and amen.

CAROL ANN BOYD

DIVINE PROTECTION

Today, many people put their trust in carnal means of protection, but Psalm 91:1 declares, "He that dwelleth in the secret place of the Most-High shall abide under the shadow of the Almighty."

~ Let us Pray ~

Lord, you rule heaven and earth. You are always our faithful God and our divine protector. Out of the abundance of our beings, and out of the depths of our souls, we cry to you. Lord, you hear the cry of the righteous. You hear and answer us.

We are currently experiencing unprecedented times of uncertainty and anxiety. We ask you to calm our anxieties and teach us to be anxious about nothing and pray about everything. You are our strong deliverer.

When the enemy comes in like a flood, you are the Almighty, the righteous, and the highest judge. You issue a restraining order against our enemy. The word of God states, "Let God arise, let his enemies be scattered: let them also that hate him flee before him" (Psalm 68:1 KJV). Lord, please be a fence around us every day. Be our rock of defense, our shield, and our buckler. Sanctify us through your word. Your word is

CAROL ANN BOYD

truth. Let your word be in our mouths to bless you at all times. Let your word be a light unto our pathway and a guide unto our feet.

Almighty God, please chart our course and help us navigate through pathless seas and deep waters. You sustain us when our problems seem insurmountable. When doors close, you open new ones. You make ways out of no way. You are God of the valleys, and God of the mountains. When we are weak, you are strong. We can do all things because of Christ. Thank you for being our waymaker and eternal provider and always our divine protector. This day, the glory is thine, the power is thine, and the victory is thine. We honor you in Jesus's name. Amen.

WELFARE OF CHILDREN

Children are special to God. He places great emphasis on and shows great concern for their well-being.

> And they brought young children to him, that he should touch them: and his disciples rebuked those that brought them. But when Jesus saw it, he was much displeased, and said unto them, suffer the little children to come unto me, and forbid them not: for of such is the kingdom of God. Verily I say unto you, whosoever shall not receive the kingdom of God as a little child, he shall not enter therein. And he took them up in his arms, put his hands upon them, and blessed them. (Mark 10:13–16 KJV)

CAROL ANN BOYD

~ Let us Pray ~

Father, in your mighty name, we give you thanks this day! Thank you for the children you have given to us and put in our care as mothers, fathers, grandparents, and caregivers. Thank you for loving the children that are homeless, abused, and hospitalized. May we be blessed to provide financial blessings for children that are victims of cancer and various diseases.

Thank you for the teachers who instruct and guide our children daily. We ask you, Lord, for your hand of protection for the children as they walk to school and ride school buses. Lord, please protect them as they arrive at daycares, school campuses, and churches.

Lord, be a fence around them every day. Keep back the powers of Satan, the wicked one who enters the hearts of men and women to kill and destroy their lives. Lord Jesus, today, bring down the enemy's plot to hurt and harm innocent victims on school grounds. We also pray for the release of children that have been separated from their parents and put in cages like animals.

Thank you for your divine provisions of food, shelter, clothing, and peace to all children. Lord Jesus, let the children come to you. Wrap them safely in your arms. May the children love you, serve you, and keep you in their hearts forever. We give you all the glory and all the honor now. In Jesus name, amen and amen.

THANKING GOD FOR STRENGTH

There are times in our lives when our strength is challenged, but the bible admonishes us to be strong in the Lord and the power of his might.

~ Let us Pray ~

Lord God Almighty, I thank you for strength and quiet peace. In quietness and confidence, I have your strength. When the storms of life are raging, you stand by me. You come to me in the twilight of the evening, in the black of midnight, and in the dark hours of distress.

You come to me in a new dawn. I am safe in your arms. I am at peace. I am strong. When my body is weak, my spirit is strong. I look to you because I need you, and I know no other help.

You are very high, and you are very great. You sit high and look low. You see us in our helpless states. You reach down and lift us above the dark clouds of time. You cause the sun to shine in our hearts, and we are helped this day. Because we wait on you, our strength is renewed. We bless your great name, Jesus. Amen and amen.

CAROL ANN BOYD

PROPHETIC PRAYER OF PROSPERITY

Merriam-Webster defines prosperity as the condition of being successful or thriving. God desires that we prosper in all things.

> **Beloved, I wish above all things that thou mayest prosper and be in health, even as thy soul prospereth. (3 John 1:2 KJV)**

~ Let us Pray ~

Jesus, we bless your high and holy name! We declare that this day, where doors have closed, new doors will open.

Lord, by the authority of your high name, we cancel every plot and scheme that Satan devised against us. We declare, according to your word, that no weapon formed against us shall prosper. We speak life into every dead situation. We speak prophetically into our lives, we declare, according to your word, we are the head and not the tail.

Because we serve you in the beauty of holiness every day, our families are blessed, our children are blessed, our ministries prosper, and our witness is effective. Our spiritual growth is improved through the study of thy word.

We declare our bodies are healed from sickness and disease. Relationships, lost jobs, hopes, and dreams are restored. Much-needed peace is granted,

CAROL ANN BOYD

and anxieties are calmed. Our finances are improved, and our debts are canceled. Our desires are fulfilled according to your perfect will. And so on this day, we give you all the glory and honor that is due to your great name, Jesus. Amen and amen.

PRAYER FOR VICTIMS OF A STORM

~ Let us Pray ~

Today we pray for those who suffer the loss of homes, business establishments, and loved ones because of perilous storms, floods, and other natural disasters. They are faced with unforeseen calamities and devastation. This chaos is far beyond their control, and many are emotionally distraught.

We pray that our faithful God, who brings cosmos out of chaos, will bring peace in the midst of the storms and embrace all who suffer with his strength.

May we, as a community, continue to rise up and work together to help our neighbors. We will continue to support them by giving and contributing to their special needs. Now may the God of truth, grace, and mercy be a present help in troubled times. To God be all the glory and honor. We pray in Jesus name. Amen and amen!

CAROL ANN BOYD

PRAYER FOR MARRIAGES AND FAMILIES

God's first institution was the family; a strong unified body. He structured the family to reflect his glory. From the very beginning, Satan's plot has been to deceive man and destroy what God had ordained.

~ Let us Pray ~

Lord, we pray for families! You ordained and instituted marriage. You stated that a man should leave his father and mother and cleave to his wife. You said men should be fruitful, multiply and replenish the earth.

Satan works against your plans, and he promotes divorce and abortion. When marriages are on the rocks, we pray that spouses who are overwhelmed and facing great challenges go to the rock that is higher than they are. We pray, Lord, for you to hide them in the cleft of the rock. Help them to be committed to each other and the foundation you have instituted. May they find the love of Christ, and allow it to lead them and manifest that same love for their children.

Please heal and restore family relationships and lost hopes and dreams. Destroy the enemy's plot to steal, kill, and destroy. Foil his plot to do anything contrary to your design. Let your institution be as you orchestrated. Let there be peace and harmony between husbands, wives, and children. We glorify you this very hour and day, in the matchless name of Jesus we pray. Amen and amen.

PRAYER FOR LOCAL AND INTERNATIONAL GOVERNMENTS

I exhort therefore, that, first of all, supplications, prayers, intercessions, and giving of thanks, be made for all men; For kings, and for all that are in authority; that we may lead a quiet and peaceable life in all godliness and honesty. For this is good and acceptable in the sight of God our Saviour; Who will have all men to be saved, and to come unto the knowledge of the truth. (1 Timothy 2:1–4 KJV)

~ Let us Pray ~

Lord, we pray that you will guide the president of the United States, all world leaders, and all local and state government officials. We pray that all leaders, advisors, and judges will turn to you for direction. We pray for them to have their people at heart and to not try to control their people's lives but make every citizen's life better.

We pray for those in other countries that are suffering mentally, physically, and financially. You are the God of every nation, and we bless your name. To God be glory and honor in Jesus name. Amen and amen.

The Speaker's Source

> Then Abigail made haste and took
> two hundred loaves, two bottles of
> wine, five sheep ready dressed, five
> measures of parched corn, a hundred
> clusters of raisins, and two hundred
> cakes of figs, and laid them on asses.
> (1 Samuel 25:18 KJV)

A servant said to the wise woman, Abigail, **"Now, therefore, know and consider what thou wilt do; for evil is determined against our master, and against all his household: for he is such a son of Belial, that a man cannot speak to him" (1 Samuel 25:17 KJV)**. The message of imminent danger was clear: it's going down tonight! Abigail is informed and empowered because when you don't know, you are powerless. **"My people are destroyed for the lack of knowledge" (Hosea 4:6 KJV)**. Abigail has been informed, and now she has the power to stop mass murder.

The servant's instructions to Abigail were clear: consider and make your move. The ball is in your court.

> For if any be a hearer of the word and not a doer, he is like unto a man beholding his natural face in a glass: For he beholdeth himself, and goeth his way, and straightway forgetteth what manner of man he was. But whoso looketh into the perfect law of liberty, and continueth therein, he being not a forgetful hearer, but a doer of the work, this man shall be blessed in his deed. (James 1:23–25 KJV)

Inaction is not an option, and a plan without action is empty, like faith without works is dead. Procrastination is never an option, especially in a crisis.

When you hear a warning, govern yourself accordingly. Abigail's wealth and beauty were irrelevant. David was still angry and was going to kill Nabal for refusing to feed him. Nabal referred to David as a runaway slave. David, however, was secretly an anointed king, a shepherd boy, skilled with a sling, a warrior, and a skilled musician.

When we are in a crisis, our status does not matter. *(Satan does not care if we are healthy, wealthy, and wise.)* It does not matter whether we are doctors, lawyers, professors, or bishops. Satan seeks to destroy us and bring us down.

David didn't care that he was rich, had servants, or owned a city. He wanted to be fed. "Fed" is the operative word.

Your position does not matter in a crisis. So get off your high horse and come down from your ivory tower. Dismount, bow, and submit.

Abigail listened and took immediate action. She made a decision, formulated a plan, and prepared food. She became an intercessor. She took action.

CAROL ANN BOYD

She had the advantage of counseling David, and the resource she had at hand was food. Most importantly, she had wisdom. She prepared to confront her enemy. "If thine enemy hunger, feed him."

The Command Performance consists of:

1. Bowing (a paradigm shift)
2. The intercessory speech

Note the word haste is used three times in 1 Samuel, in 25:18, 23, and 34, because "procrastination is a thief of time." Yes, haste makes waste!

Mission accomplished! David's anger was abated by Abigail. He accepted her wise counsel. Nabal had a stroke; he was killed by God. Then David married Abigail. The result was a happy and beneficial ending for Abigail.

The discretion of a man deferreth his anger, and it is his glory to pass over a transgression. (Proverbs 19:11 KJV)

Abigail thought on her feet and was quick to act. There should be no hesitation in crisis. Though Abigail sounded like she was flattering David and buttering him up, she was ingenious. Her dilemma called for strategy, not flattery. We must do what we have to do.

So when they had dined, Jesus saith to Simon Peter, Simon, son of Jonas, lovest thou me more than these? He saith unto him, Yea, Lord; thou knowest that I love thee. He saith unto him, Feed my lambs. He saith to him again the second time, Simon, son of Jonas, lovest thou me? He saith unto him, Yea, Lord; thou knowest that I love thee. He saith unto him, Feed my sheep. He saith unto him the third time, Simon, son of Jonas, lovest thou me? Peter was grieved because he said unto the third time, Lovest thou me? And he said unto him, Lord, thou knowest all things; thou knowest that I love thee. Jesus saith unto him, Feed my sheep. Verily, verily, I say unto

thee, when thou wast young, thou girdedst thyself, and walkedst whither thou wouldest: but when thou shalt be old, thou shalt stretch forth thy hands, and another shall gird thee, and carry thee whither thou wouldest not. This spake he, signifying by what death he should glorify God. And when he had spoken this, he saith unto him, follow me. (John 21:15–19 KJV)

To feed means to deposit into continuously; to furnish something essential to development, sustenance maintenance, or operation of; or to satisfy, gratify, support, or encourage.

Jesus thought that this was most important, imperative, and relevant. Feed is the operative word; the working word. Consequently, when we are fed the word of God, we receive what we need, and we are privileged to become conduits.

A conduit is a natural or artificial channel through

which something such as fluid is conveyed; a means of transmitting or distributing; or *a leader.*

So what exactly is the "feeding" that Jesus described? Hold your bibles up.

It is the word of God that feeds us, for it is the way to a man's heart.

ON THE BRINK OF VICTORY

Merriam-Webster's definition of brink is the point that is very close to the occurrence of something very good or bad. Use what is at your disposal. (Moses used his staff.)

> **And the Lord said unto him, what is that in thine hand? And he said, a rod. (Exodus 4:2 KJV)**
>
> **And thou shalt take this rod in thine hand, wherewith thou shalt do signs. (Exodus 4:17 KJV)**

And Moses took his wife and his sons, and set them upon an ass, and he returned to the land of Egypt: and Moses took the rod of God in his hand. (Exodus 4:20 KJV)

And the Lord said unto Moses, Wherefore criest thou unto me? Speak unto the children of Israel, that they go forward: But lift thou up thy rod, and stretch out thine hand over the sea, and divide it: and the children of Israel shall go on dry ground through the midst of the sea. (Exodus 14:15–16 KJV)

Stay the course. Keep marching around insurmountable walls. They will fall.

And ye shall compass the city, all ye men of war, and go round about the city once. Thus, shalt thou do six days. And seven priests shall bear before the ark seven trumpets of rams' horns: and the seventh day ye shall compass the city seven times, and the priests shall blow with the trumpets. And it shall come to pass, that when they make a long blast with the ram's horn, and when ye hear the sound of the trumpet, all the people shall shout; and the wall of the city shall fall down flat, and the people shall ascend up every man straight before him. (Joshua 6:3–5 KJV)

So the people shouted when the priests blew with the trumpets: and it came to pass, when the people heard the sound of the trumpet, and the people shouted with a great shout, that the wall fell down flat, so that the people went up into the city, every man straight before him, and they took the city. (Joshua 6:20 KJV)

Jehoshaphat just sang and praised God. The battle belongs to God.

And he said, hearken ye, all Judah, and ye inhabitants of Jerusalem, and thou king Jehoshaphat, thus saith Lord unto you, be not afraid nor dismayed by reason of this great multitude; for the battle is not yours, but God's. (2 Chronicles 20:15 KJV)

Ye shall not need to fight in this battle: set yourselves, stand ye still, and see the salvation of the Lord with you, O Judah and Jerusalem: fear not, nor be dismayed; tomorrow go out against them: for the Lord will be with you. (2 Chronicles 20:17 KJV)

And when he had consulted with the people, he appointed singers unto the Lord, and that should praise the beauty of holiness, as they went out before the army, and to say, Praise the Lord; for his mercy endureth forever. And when they began to sing and to praise, the Lord set ambushments against the children of Ammon, Moab, and mount Seir, which were come against Judah; and they were smitten. (2 Chronicles 20:21–22 KJV)

THE SCARLET THREAD

The first messianic promise is mentioned in Genesis 3:15. Rahab is listed in the genealogy of Jesus in the first chapter of Matthew and in The Faith Hall of Fame in the book of Hebrews. She was not condemned for her life but commended for her faith in the God of Israel.

The scarlet thread is a central theme in the book of Joshua and throughout the bible as a whole. The story of Rahab and the scarlet thread foretold redemption for the faithful. Blood is the key element in our salvation. This blood-red rope is a type of blood-red scarlet thread that is mentioned throughout the bible, from Genesis to Revelation.

> **For the life of the flesh is in the blood: and I have given it to you upon the altar to make an atonement for your souls: for it is the blood that**

maketh an atonement for the soul.
(Leviticus 17:11 KJV)

In whom we have redemption through
his blood, even the forgiveness of sins.
(Colossians 1:14 KJV)

Unto Adam also and to his wife did
the Lord God make coats of skins and
clothed them. (Genesis 3:21 KJV)

God shed innocent blood to cover the sin of Adam
and Eve by making them clothes from animal skins.
This is a picture of the covering of righteousness that
we receive when the Lord Jesus Christ died for us.

And they shall take of the blood and
strike it on the two side posts and on the
upper door post of the houses, wherein
they shall eat it. (Exodus 12:7 KJV)

Moses told the Hebrews to put the shed blood of
a lamb on the two side posts and on the upper door

post" of their houses. God said, **"And the blood will be a sign for you on the houses where you are; and when I see the blood, I will pass over you, and the plague shall not be upon you to destroy you, when I smite the land of Egypt."** (Exodus 12:13 KJV)

> For I have received of the Lord that which also I delivered unto, that the Lord Jesus the same night in which he was betrayed took bread: And when he had given thanks, he brake it, and said, Take, eat: this is my body, which is broken for you: this do in remembrance of me. After the same manner also he took the cup, when he had supped, saying, this cup is the new testament in my blood: this do ye, as oft as ye drink it, in remembrance of me. For as often as ye eat this bread, and drink the cup, ye do shew the Lord's death till he come. (1 Corinthians 11:23–26 KJV)

In the Lord's Supper prayer, Paul mentions the two elements that remind us of what Jesus did for us. Firstly, the bread which represents Jesus's broken body. Secondly, the cup, which represents Jesus's shed blood.

In fact, during biblical times, the law required that nearly ever ything be cleansed with blood. Without the shedding of blood, there is no forgiveness.

> **And almost all things are by the law purged with blood; and without shedding blood is no remission. (Hebrews 9:22 KJV)**

> **Whom God hath set forth to be a propitiation through faith in his blood, to declare his righteousness for the remission of sins that are past, through the forbearance of God. (Romans 3:25 KJV)**

God presented Christ as a sacrifice for atonement through the shedding of his blood, only to be received by faith.

And he is the head of the body, the church: who is the beginning, the firstborn from the dead; that in all things he might have the preeminence. For it pleased the Father that in him should all fulness dwell; And, having made peace through the blood of his cross, by him to reconcile all things unto himself; by him, I say, whether they be things in earth, or things in heaven. (Colossians 1:18–20 KJV)

But if we walk in the light, as he is in the light, we have fellowship one with another, and the blood of Jesus Christ his Son cleanseth us from all sin. (1 John 1:7 KJV)

The blood of Jesus purifies us from all sin if we walk in the light because he is in the light.

Forasmuch as ye know that ye were not redeemed with corruptible things, as silver and gold, from your vain conversation received by tradition from your fathers; But with the precious blood of Christ, as of a lamb without blemish and without spot: (1 Peter 1:18–19 KJV)

Rahab was a harlot who lived in Jericho in the Promised Land and assisted the Israelites in capturing the city. After escaping, the spies promised to spare Rahab and her family after they took city if she would mark her house by hanging a red cord out the window.

Rahab moved forward because of the scarlet thread of redemption in her window. She is an ancestor of Jesus Christ. As she moved forward, she gained a vision of a new purposeful life, a new gig, a new walk, and a new talk that was far better than prostitution (Matthew 1:1–16 KJV).

PRAYER CHANGES THINGS

Prayer not only changes our situations, but prayer changes the one who prays. The first mention of prayer in the scripture is found in Genesis 4:26, which states, "then men began to call on the name of the Lord." Things were happening for people that allowed them to call on the Lord. What things? How did the people know to pray? They knew because they were taught. When the disciples asked to be taught to pray as John's disciples, Jesus taught them.

THE STYLE OF PRAYER

The Lord expressed the manner in which we should pray in (Matthew 6:9–13 KJV).

- Clearly direct your prayer: "Our father who art in heaven,"
- Praise God before making your request: "hallowed be thy name,"
- Seek God's kingdom and his will: "thy kingdom come, thy will be done in earth as it is in heaven."

- Petition God for daily spiritual sustenance: "Give us this day our daily bread,"
- Seek God's forgiveness: "and forgive us our debts, as we forgive our debtors,"
- Ask God for divine guidance and deliverance: "and lead us not into temptation, but deliver us from evil,"
- End with praise: "for thine is the kingdom, and the power, and the glory, forever. Amen."

God created man in his image and placed in him a soul that would long for and cry out to the living God.

As the hart panteth after the water brook, so panteth my soul after thee oh God. (Psalm 42:1 KJV)

Even men in a drunken stupor cry out to God. What has to happen today for men to begin to call on the name of the Lord?

God said his house shall be called a house of prayer (not a fish fry, cookout, restaurant, or social club).

There are things happening now that should cause men to call on the Lord. Sadly, even though we are taught we should pray, we are living in a most unprecedented and horrific time of sickness, depression, oppression, social injustice and deceit, diabolical and deliberate police brutality, egregious sin, and debauchery.

God is able to and will bring cosmos out of chaos, but he can't do so by us just going through routine church activities. The people of God must humble themselves and pray (2 Chronicles 7:14 KJV). Prayer is not just talking to God but an indicator of humility. You bow before him.

We are prone to judge, but it is possible to ascertain a person's prayer life by their lifestyle and speech. Some things just go together, like prayer and God's word or prayer and faith, but we must incorporate works with faith. For without the works it is dead. So work it! Work it!

The words of a song are building blocks. But for what? **Jude 1:20 says, "But ye beloved, building up yourselves on your most holy faith, praying in the Holy Ghost."** You cannot be built without prayer.

Special Feature

My husband taught that prayer is not meant to change God, but rather it is meant to change the person that is praying. When you pray, there will be a change in your spirit, attitude, and conduct. Prayer will also bring about a clear change in your countenance, such as when Moses came down from the mountain after he had been in lengthy communication with God.

> **And it came to pass, when Moses came down from mount Sinai with the two tables of testimony in Moses' hand, when he came down from the mount, that Moses wist not that the skin of his face shone while he talked with him. And when Aaron and all the children of Israel saw Moses, behold, the skin of his face shone; and they were afraid to come nigh him. (Exodus 34:29–30 KJV)**

My husband taught a certain bible class one day. He emphasized that prayer is about releasing God's energy. *What do you mean?* I mused. As I began to meditate on this lesson, the Lord gave me a great revelation. I later taught my own bible class titled "Releasing Water in the Building."

RELEASING GOD'S ENERGY

In my class, I was able to expound on this lesson to illustrate how God's energy is released. Energy is the spiritual force that flows through the people of God. However, we must realize that God is not a fairy tale or magic genie where you can rub a lamp, and say *do what I say.* Then tell him to get back in the lamp. There must be action on the part of God's children to release his energy. What is that action? Faith.

Let me illustrate this. Water, a necessary commodity, is in a building, though you cannot see it. When the blueprints of a house are drawn, waterlines are added for showers, tubs, sinks, and water fountains.

When one desires to bathe or get a drink of water,

they do not call a plumber. Running water is already equipped in the house. One already has the resources that allow them to release the water. We step on the pedal at a water fountain. We lift or turn on a water faucet. These actions release the water.

We, the people of God, already have the resources that we need to release God's energy.

> **According as his divine power hath given unto us all things that pertain unto life and godliness, through the knowledge of him that hath called us to glory and virtue: (2 Peter 1:3 KJV)**

> **Jesus said unto him, If thou canst believe, all things are possible to him that believeth. (Mark 9:23 KJV)**

So the action that releases God's energy to us is faith.

> **Faith cometh by hearing, and hearing by the word of God. (Romans 10:17 KJV)**

He that cometh to God must believe that he is, and that he is a rewarder of them that diligently seek him. (Hebrew 11:6 KJV)

Why stand at the water fountain and do nothing? Why stand there and refuse to turn the handle or step on the pedal?

When faucets are turned, handles lifted, and pedals stepped on, valves that you cannot see are opened and water issues forth. It is released and begins flowing through the pipes. When one activates their faith, heaven's resources open. They are never exhausted, and the benefits of God's great power are released to you.

The first power source is the Holy Ghost power; the power to become the sons of God.

But ye shall receive power, after that the Holy Ghost is come upon you: and ye shall be witnesses unto me both in Jerusalem, and in all Judaea, and

Samaria, and unto the uttermost part of the earth. (Acts 1:8 KJV)

But as many as received him, to them gave he the power to become the sons of God, even to them that believe on his name. (St. John 1:12 KJV)

And they were all filled with the Holy Ghost, and began to speak with other tongues, as the Spirit gave them utterance. (Acts 2:4 KJV)

The second power source is the efficacious blood of Jesus. It has redeeming properties; it covers, protects, heals, purifies, and restores our souls and eradicates sin. It never loses its power. It is never exhausted. Thank God that the blood prevails.

REGULATING THE RELEASE

How far you stretch your faith determines how much of God's energy is released to you. Do you want a drop of water? A cup? Pint? Quart? Gallon? Or would you rather have a steady stream of water that overflows? Bishop used to pray all the time to let faith come alive. Let faith become activated, because faith without action is nothing.

There are times that we may incur plumbing problems in our homes. Sinks and toilets may become clogged, and we have to call a plumber. However, when our spiritual life encounters problems or gets clogged, we call on a power source—the blood of Jesus. There is power in the blood. We plead the blood, and it still works. So we just plead the blood.

The efficacious blood will fix your problems. It will adjust and restore. Jesus will fix things for you, he knows just what to do. So, whenever you pray, let him have his way, for he will fix things for you. His efficacious blood will reach you and do what it is designed to do. So pray, pray, pray!

King with a
Sling and a Stone

Goliath, the Philistine champion, had heavy and powerful weapons. So King Saul presented David with armor to bring down the Philistine, however, David refused it because King Saul's weapon had not been proven or tried. David used what was tried, sure, and effective; a stone. He brought Goliath down with one smooth stone.

David, son of Jesse, was a shepherd, a skilled musician, a warrior with a sling, and an anointed and appointed king. He said, **"And David spake to the men that stood by him, saying, what shall be done to the man that killeth this Philistine, and taketh away the reproach from Israel? for who is this uncircumcised Philistine, that he should defy the armies of the living God?" (1 Samuel 17:26 KJV).** Who is Goliath to challenge God's children to combat? Who is he to question and confront the armies of the living God?

David was small but mighty, and a force to be

reckoned with. He hurled the stone and didn't miss. Goliath said he would feed David's flesh to the fowls of the air. David said Goliath had it twisted. He was going to feed Goliath to the fowls of the air. He does not run from Goliath but toward him. And with one quick assiduous, meticulous throw with a sling, he hurls a stone and knocks the giant out.

> And Saul armed David with his armour, and he put a helmet of brass upon his head; also he armed him with a coat of mail. And David girded his sword upon his armour, and he assayed to go; for he had not proved it. And David said unto Saul, I cannot go with these; for I have not proved them. And David put them off him. And he took his staff in his hand, and chose him five smooth stones out of the brook, and put them in a shepherd's bag which he had, even in a scrip; and his sling was in his hand: and he drew near to the Philistine (1 Samuel 17:38–40 KJV)

The people of God are winners in battle when they use the same thing to bring down giants in their lives today. David used a quick smooth stone and knocked the giant's brains out. We still use a stone. Jesus is that stone hewed out of the mountain. Therefore, use the same thing that David used—a stone!

> **Therefore, thus saith the Lord God, Behold, I lay in Zion for a foundation a stone, a "TRIED" stone, a precious cornerstone, a sure foundation: he that believeth shall not make haste. (Isaiah 28:16 KJV)**

Today especially in the deceptive political and social media arenas and secret societies, social misfits spew lies as they go forth to deceive innocent people.

> **Be sober, be vigilant; because your adversary the devil, as a roaring lion, walketh about, seeking whom he may devour: (1 Peter 5:8 KJV)**

Today who does Satan, the liar, think he is? Who is he to roar like a lion to alarm God's people? But wait!

For God hath not given us the spirit of fear; but of power, and of love, and of a sound mind (2 Timothy 1:7 KJV)

Who is Satan to charge the people of the true and living God?

Who shall lay anything to the charge of God's elect? It is God that justifieth. (Romans 8:33 KJV)

We, the people of God, take exception to Satan, the liar, calling us out.

It is imperative that we all stand in solidarity in prayer and make it our focus. It is our weapon against every evil and every plot of Satan to overthrow God's kingdom. Satan's kingdom must come down.

WHO DO YOU THINK YOU ARE, MR. BIG STUFF?

How dare you! You deformed, ugly, ten-foot giant! Who are you to rant, rave, threaten, and manipulate God's children?

Who do you think you are, Mr. Big Stuff? The people of God ask if you want some of this. This alliance of sanctified prayer warriors, these people of the name.

This is us! Blood-bought, blood-washed, sanctified and redeemed body of baptized believers in Jesus Christ.

This is us! Children of the Most-High God, kings, and priests unto God.

This is us! The body of appointed and anointed believers in Jesus Christ.

This is us! Defenders of the gospel of peace.

This is us! Contenders for the faith once delivered to the saints.

This is us! Servants of the Ancient of Days and

special agents of The Chief Apostle—the blessed and only Potentate, the King of kings, and Lord of lords.

Satan, you are the master of evil and the forger of lies. You are a menace to society. But do not get it twisted. God has not given his people the spirit of fear but of power, love, and a sound mind.

The weapons of our warfare are not carnal. No weapon formed against us shall prosper.

Now hear this, Satan, you've been building your kingdom all over the world. Satan, you evil giant, your kingdom must come down. It has to come down! It has *got to* come down! It will come down! It is coming down! God said the high places, he would bring down.

This is us! The righteousness of God; the valiant soldiers of the cross. We are a godly force to be reckoned with. And when we make it to that city called heaven, it will be alright.

This is us! Children of the alpha and omega; the beginning and end.

This is us! Agents of his Lordship, Jesus Christ.

This is us! Water-baptized, Holy Ghost-filled, tongue-speaking, right-talking, right-walking, right-living, right-giving, right-praying, right-staying saints of the Most High God.

Ascribe ye greatness to our God!

We, the people of God, are duty-bound to give him great praise in his house, always and forever!

To the only wise God our Savior, be glory, majesty, dominion, and power, both now and forever. Amen and amen!

Special Scripture References

Mandatory Prayers

- 1 Chronicles 16:11, 24:19
- 2 Chronicles 7:14
- Isaiah 55:6
- Matthew 6:7–9
- Luke 11:12, 18:1
- Acts 12:5
- 1 Thessalonians 5:17
- Romans 1:9
- 2 Timothy 1:3
- Hebrews 4:16

Invitation to Pray

- Deuteronomy 33:26
- Psalms 27:8
- Jeremiah 33:3
- Matthew 7:7
- Mark 9:23, 11:24
- Romans 10:9–10

Attributes of God

- Omniscience (he is all-wise!): Jude 25
- Omnipresence (he is everywhere at all times): Psalms 139:7–9

Omnipotent

- God has unlimited power: Psalm 62:11

Prayers Unanswered

- Secret sins: Psalm 66:18
- Disobedience: Deuteronomy 1:8, 1:45, 14:37, 28:6
- Indifference: Proverbs 1:28
- Self-indulgence: James 4:3
- Asking amiss: James 1:6–7

Prayers Answered

- Hannah:1 Samuel 1:24–28
- Elijah:1 Kings 18:36–39
- Righteousness: Psalms 34:17–19

Soul Inspiration

- Acts 4:31

Expectation

- Jeremiah 29:11

Peace

- Isaiah 26:3

The Fall of Lucifer

- Isaiah 14:12–16
- Luke 10:18
- Ezekiel 28
- Revelations 12:7–12

CAROL ANN BOYD

ABOUT THE AUTHOR

Carol Ann Boyd is a native of Minneapolis, Minnesota. She was saved at a young age and began playing the piano for her local church at the age of ten. She is very faithful and loves the Lord with all her heart.

She later married the Honorable Bishop Melvin Boyd. Together they raised seven beautiful children.

Boyd worked diligently by her husband's side as he pastored the church and ministered to the community at large. She served with excellence as the minister of music, church organist, choir director, Sunday school teacher, and assisted in other areas as needed. She also wrote several songs and spoke at various events, as she was known as an eloquent orator of the word of God. She believed in using her many gifts and talents to bless the house of God.

However, it was during one of her husband's sermons that she felt inspired to write the first of many poems. After writing over fifteen poems in one month, she realized this was another gift from God.

In 2004, she published her first book, a collection of poems titled *Inside Perceptions*. Each poem is a reflection of relatable experiences and her deep devotion to the things of God. Now here she is again, writing at age seventy-eight, but this time with a passion for prayer. She encourages others to connect with God. Amazingly, she writes during a time of great racial hatred, pain, despair, and utter chaos, but is yet trusting God.

Enter her thought patterns to see how she connects to the loving Creator. You will be inspired.

Printed in the United States
by Baker & Taylor Publisher Services